A Week in the Life of Goo

COLIN MORRIS

A Week in the Life of God

If God kept a diary . . .

EPWORTH PRESS

7162 0430 4

First published 1986
by Epworth Press
Room 195, 1 Central Buildings
Westminster, London SW1H 9NR

Printed in Great Britain by
Richard Clay (The Chaucer Press) Ltd
Bungay, Suffolk

In happy memory of
Robert Foxcroft

ACKNOWLEDGMENTS

I am grateful for the courtesy, enthusiasm and shrewdness of John Stacey, Chairman of the Epworth Press. I also owe much to Annie Proctor who typed the manuscript and the *Thoughts for the Day* on which it is based, and through lively discussion helped to clarify and sharpen my ideas.

INTRODUCTION

On the Problems of Playing at God

Not that you ever doubted it, but let me assure you anyway that it is very hard work indeed playing at God. It's this business of trying to be fair to everybody. Any parent with a clutch of children knows the problem. Hence, doing the decent thing by the three billion inhabitants of this little old planet is no mean task, especially since the arithmetic is such that if God intervenes on behalf of a single member of the human race, he then has trillions upon trillions of other relationships to adjust.

And God must not only be fair but also wise, and the divine wisdom is bound to be inscrutable in all sorts of ways. Somewhere in these pages God exhorts his children not to think human thoughts divinely but to think divine thoughts humanly. That's what Jesus did, and half the time his contemporaries could make neither head nor tail of what he was saying or else they thought he was off his head. It was the radical otherness of his ideas that jarred, not their conventional cleverness or worldly profundity. Since God insists that his thoughts are not our thoughts, things must look so different from the Godward side of reality that any attempt to put those thoughts into words ought to sound more like gobbledegook than extracts from the *Oxford Book of Quotations*.

One thing is for sure – to play God, not frivolously, doling out blessings and curses at a whim, but seriously, paying attention to the rules of the game – is a spiritually demanding, intellectually taxing and theologically hair-raising exercise. It is so fraught with the risk of blasphemy as to make one nervous

1

about venturing out of doors in a thunderstorm for fear of being struck by lightning. It also cures one of any tendency to give vent to such casual incantations as 'God willing!' These pietistic ejaculations lose much of their primitive charm when one is committed to working out precisely what they mean. How can God be 'willing' or otherwise for *anyone* to do *anything*, and what happens if he isn't? How does God put the skids under any human endeavour since he has forsworn the use of legions of angels as a heavenly constabulary?

So why do it? Why try to play at God? This may sound an appalling confession for a minister of religion with umpteen years' experience to make, but I was curious to know more about God. *God*, not Jesus nor God *in* Jesus but God as he is in himself, unincarnated, if I dare use that word. I suppose I have become exasperated by a certain fundamentalist Jesusolatry which tries to contain God's ineffable grandeur within a framework of biblical texts about Jesus, as though what we *do* know about Jesus is all we *can* know about God. There is surely something downright provincial about the notion that the Almighty sulked in silence in the seventh heaven from the beginning of time until 4 BC or thereabouts when he decided to bestir himself and introduce himself to the human race, or at least to a tiny part of it.

None of the foregoing sentiments is intended to play down the significance of Jesus, either for Christians generally or for this Christian in particular. But against those who insist that Jesus reveals God, I want to retort that he also hides God – not by his own conscious intention but by the way his followers use him as a swingeing abridgement of God-knowledge. Ask a question about the God who is Father of our Lord Jesus Christ and back like a pistol shot comes some biblical text that speaks of the one who left footprints in the sand of Palestine, spoke in human if enigmatic language and behaved like a Galilean workman. That, says the Jesusolators, is all you need know about God. Seek no further. Behold, Jesus! Jesus is God's analogue – project onwards and upwards from Jesus, multiply

2

by the power X and there, looming ahead, is the Ancient of Days.

I am well aware that respectful agnosticism about the God who is behind and beyond Jesus is enjoined on all Christians, but I have it on the best of authority that Jesusolatry will not do: the authority of Jesus himself. He pointed away from himself towards the God whom he worshipped and compared to whom, he said, not even he deserved to be called good. 'Don't look at me, look at him!' he declared. Now if Jesus would not allow himself to stand in God's light, we would do well to copy his diffidence and avoid the trap of a lazy Jesus cultus which side-steps all the big questions about God's nature and purposes by sheltering behind a handful of well-loved biblical texts.

It is not only some fundamentalists who seem to prefer sharp-edged if limited knowledge of God to an encounter with the boundless mystery that bursts out of our vocabulary and eludes our attempts to label it. The theological radicals also have their pet forms of reductionism. They talk of Jesus 'as the human face of God' and as the lens through which we may gaze into the heart of God. Indubitably true sentiments but plainly inadequate as formulae for circumscribing the Deity. They cannot be good enough for us because they would certainly not have been good for that unflinching monotheist, Jesus of Nazareth. 'No other Gods!' he declared. Not even . . . Jesus?

I do believe that every Christian needs from time to time a dose of thoroughgoing monotheism to clean out his clogged theological system, thus keeping his soul healthy and his feet on the right track, following Jesus in the quest for his Father's Kingdom. And who better to administer that cathartic medicine to the bemused Christian than the Jews? He who wishes to learn about God, or at least to discover in detail the ways in which God is unknowable, must go either to the Jews or their first cousins the Muslims, whose fierce protection of God's holiness is one of the religious glories of a secular age. The Jews, of course, have the additional qualification that they

3

taught the young Jesus about God, and even the most un-ashamed but open-minded sceptic would perhaps concede that they made a good job of it.

So I went to the Jews, whose bare survival is the most majestic testimony to God's existence that history offers, though 'existence' is too bloodless and abstract a word for the rich, colourful skein of legend, parable and proverb that the Jews have woven around God's being. I poked about in that treasure house of spirituality, the Tales of the Hasidim, and made the acquaintance of vibrant and holy men such as Nachman of Bratslav, the Maggid of Dubno and Israel ben Elieser, the Polish lime burner turned evangelist who was John Wesley's contemporary and had a similar power to rejuvenate flagging faith and excite such religious zeal that 'Jews fell in love with the Lord and felt such yearning for God that it was unbearable. ...' The Baal Shem also seems to have shared Wesley's capacity for infuriating the religious establishment and getting himself thrown out of places of worship.

Then there is the *Haggadah*, a huge repository of folklore and fables *and* the *Pirke Abot*, the Sayings of the Fathers, *and The Duties of the Heart and* Maimonides' Code *and* on and on ... a mountain of precious truth, much of it in the form of pithy sayings that are easily memorable and therefore completely portable. Just as there was a time during the Ottoman Empire when the Turkish Foreign Minister kept his documents in saddlebags in case he had to skidaddle, so the Jewish people, conditioned to catastrophe, hid their treasure where thieves could not break in and steal, in their memories; luggage that took up no space; jewels in the mind, beyond the reach of predators.

And much of this rabbinical lore is taken up with God – his nature, attributes, habits, likes and dislikes and snatches of conversation with his servants, the rabbis. This is a curious thing, that a people whose religious genius rests on the un-flinching insistence that God's being is utterly private and not to be captured in any image, superscription or picture, should

4

tell tales about him that are often rudely familiar and always warmly sensuous. I suspect this is cause and effect. Because the Jews' religion is founded on the great rock of God's holiness, they feel free to frolic around the edges, like children on their father's knee, gently mocking his great strength but without disrespect. Or to change the image, if you lark about in a rowing boat, you risk sinking it, but you can bounce up and down on the deck of an ocean liner without causing a tremor – and the Jewish understanding of the nature of God is a great deep-sea Leviathan of a faith.

So any budding rabbinical students who read these pages could well divert themselves with an ecclesiastical version of a newspaper Spot-the-Ball competition – 'Name that Rabbi!' – for a number of these entries have been inspired by Jewish wisdom. But not all, for Judaism is not a sacerdotal religion, hag-ridden by priests. The God-intoxication of the Jews permeates every level of society and not just those fastnesses occupied by professionals who earn their living from the teaching of theology or the service of the synagogue. Jewish comedians such as Woody Allen, Mel Brooks and Leo Rosten are also amongst the sages. Especially Jehovah's favourite wit, Woody Allen, for whom God and sex are twin preoccupations. Like a demented faun he gambols along the boundary line between piety and impertinence: 'I wish God would give me a clear sign of his existence. Like depositing a large sum in my name in a Swiss bank account', he cries, or, 'I don't want to achieve immortality through my work, I want to achieve it through not dying', or, 'I don't believe in an afterlife but I'm bringing along a change of underwear just in case.' That is the natural man joking in the face of the ultimately serious or railing with hopeless bravado against his fate like the Psalmist on a bad day.

But not only the rabbis and Jewish wits joust with Jehovah. The average Jewish momma is a veritable firecracker of *bon mots* about a God who is not confined to the realm of metaphysics but is up to his divine neck in the everyday business of

5

cooking, child-rearing and the social observances of the respectable Jewish family. So pervasive has been the Jewish mother's influence that according to the Talmud, whenever Rab Joseph heard the approaching step of his mother, he would say, 'I must stand up, for the *shekhinah* (God's glory) enters.'

I was taught by godly men at theological college that anthropomorphism – giving God human attributes – is a horrid sin, but my encounters with Jewish wisdom have convinced me that any God who exudes warmth as well as light will develop some persona anyway. It is not easy for the average person to emote about philosophical propositions or burn with love for a formless, impassible being who is everywhere and nowhere at the same time. Of course, Christians could justifiably retort that if one is to be anthropomorphic about God, one may as well settle for Jesus and be done with it. But it seems to me immensely significant for the purity as well as truth of proper religion that the Jews managed to invest God with all manner of warm and lovable qualities without succumbing to the living idolatry of a human representation.

And yet ... in spite of my sternest efforts, Jesus will keep insinuating himself into the entries in this diary. I suppose this fact must speak of the inevitability *for* me of the Christian way of looking at God. Try as I might, puzzle as hard as I may, there are aspects of the nature and action of God that do not make sense to me except in the light of the Christian revelation. I find this immensely reassuring. Were I able, imaginatively, to enter into the life of God for a space and not hear echoes of the voice of Jesus or reverberations of his actions, I would be a very worried believer and an even more jittery minister of the Christian religion. But if anything in this book is accounted as Christian testimony, it is testimony of the last resort; Christian truth squeezing through the key-hole after I had done everything to seal the doors and windows against it. Yet testimony of the last resort has its own peculiar power like a death-bed confession or the expression of reluctant admiration that passes the lips when an opponent whom one desperately wants to beat plays a brilliant stroke.

A word about humour. God's diary is replete with terrible jokes, and to say that obviously God has a sense of humour is a cop-out. The big brains claim that all humour has its roots in discrepancy, the gap between what is and what ought to be. Freud wrote about the discrepancy between the super-ego and the libido; the philosopher Bergson, of the discrepancy between the human organism and the mechanical world. This would certainly explain the wonderful tradition of Jewish humour, for they are a people whose whole history has been one of incongruity, the tragic discrepancy between what they had the right to expect and what actually befell them. That is a gap as wide, say, as the trenches in which they buried the dead at Auchswitz. Thus could one Jewish inmate of Belsen say to another: 'Given a life like this, death is really no misfortune. I think sometimes it would be better for a Jew not to have been born at all.' 'True,' the other nodded, 'But how many Jews are that lucky? Maybe one in ten thousand!'

Victor Frankel, an Austrian Jewish psychiatrist, wrote of his experiences in a Nazi extermination camp. He describes how the inmates passed beyond terror to the point where every morning when the commandant appeared with the dreaded list in his hand of those chosen for the gas chambers, the victims found themselves laughing out loud at the portentousness of this daily ritual and the officer's ludicrous mispronunciation of their names. It was not hysteria, Frankel insisted, but laughter as a strategy; the only way children of God brutalized like animals could assert their essential humanity. For who, in the last resort, has the greater power, the one who has life or death control over others or those who can laugh at him?

So comedy is not a frivolous thing; it reflects the imprisonment of the human spirit in the world, sometimes of its own volition, sometimes the result of a malevolent fate. It is therefore closely akin to tragedy; both are commentaries on human finitude contrasted with God's boundless hopes for his creatures.

Hence, if humour is about discrepancy, then it must be a quality close to God's heart because he presides over the ultimate discrepancy – the world as he created it and what we have made of it. So the jokes are not light relief but a quixotic commentary on the drama of our creation, fall and redemption. And the older and more dog-eared these jokes are, the closer they get to some central truth. As the saying goes, old jokes are the best jokes; they endure because they strike some chord that has been twitching since the fall of man.

Ought I to have embarked on this enterprise at all? When I used some of these entries from God's Diary as *Thoughts for the Day*, I provoked a sizeable correspondence from shocked believers who thought me irreverent and my talks blasphemous. I always listen with particular respect to my critics, so I went carefully over what I had done, and my motives for doing it. I am unrepentant. It was not presumption on my part to imagine I was privy to God's innermost thoughts; more an act of homage to the God beyond the rather circumscribed Deity I portray in these pages. For when I had honestly done my very best and addled my brain trying to achieve a degree of profundity as would do honour to God's wisdom, I succeeded only in demarcating the infinite distance between the God who is the product of our inspired or feverish imaginings and the One who is within all things but not included, outside all things but not excluded, above all things but not beyond their reach. The real thing. The ultimate One.

Whilst I would strenuously resist any suggestion of blasphemy, I freely plead guilty to propagating the odd heresy. The *odd* heresy? These pages are a veritable cornucopia of heresy – a Theological Tripos examiner's dream text. In all modesty, I do not associate myself with St Augustine's statement that 'none save great men have been the authors of heresies'. Nor do I seek refuge in the modernist heresy that there is no such thing as heresy. The boundaries of truth may be hard to define but that does not mean there are no boundaries. The question is: who has the right to demarcate them? I suspect I might fare better at the assize of the Bishop of Durham than at that of his brother Bishop of Chester; that the theological liberals are likely to be more merciful to me than the literalists; I imagine the Jews will be more magnanimous about my crasser observations than the Muslims. But these are only guesses. If we could choose our judges, we would always walk from the court free.

The Greek root of the word 'heresy' means 'to make a choice'. I have made mine. I stand with A.N. Whitehead who once declared that it was more important that a proposition should be exciting than that it should be true, because the excitement generates the essential energy which drives it on to mark out new ground in thought. I am also comforted by William Temple's dictum that it does not matter how many heretics there are in the church so long as the church itself is not heretical. And if I dare, in such illustrious company, quote from God's diary, 'Heresy is a sudden explosion of faith'. I'd like to think the odd bang might result from one or more of these entries as connections are made in the minds of believers and sparks fly – illuminating some truth shrouded in darkness.

A number of correspondents who criticized my *Thoughts for the Day* made the point that God's life could not possibly be divided into days of the week because he inhabits an eternity in which all categories of time and historical condition are meaningless. Of course. God lives in the eternal now, but we don't, and just as he moderates his will to respect the limitations of history – he doesn't blanket out time in a great burst of divine energy – so it's fair to assume any thoughts he wishes to share with us will be doled out in measures we can comprehend. He may be having all these thoughts (and an infinite number more) simultaneously in the eternal now, but I beg leave to suggest that he treats us as a mother doling out succulent morsels to her child, bit by bit, when she herself could consume the whole in one gulp. At least, that's my story and I am sticking to it.

July 1986   Colin Morris

· 1 ·

Sunday

There he goes, dozing off at morning mass as usual. I suppose I should take it as a complement that he trusts me not to get up to any mischief whilst he's asleep.

Monday

Much to-do over a bolt of lightning striking York Minster after the consecration of a bishop who has upset some folk by his views.

Some Christians are claiming the lightning strike is a sign of my disapproval. But really ... given the clouds of balderdash that have wafted heavenwards from Christian pulpits for centuries, I can't think the bishop's views are so shocking as to deserve a direct rebuke from heaven. Now, the other week, I heard a sermon from a Methodist church that really had my trigger finger itching ... But what kind of a God do they think I am? If I were angry, am I likely to take my wrath out on an inanimate object like a building? That puts me on a par with the man who, because he is cross with his wife, kicks his car when it won't start on a cold morning.

And if I were in the business of playing around with the elements in order to affect matters on earth, would I be so frivolous as to hurl thunderbolts at a bout of theological controversy and hold my hand when drought threatens to starve millions in Africa?

Tuesday

After a good start, he stumbles yet again and wants to give up the path to holiness. It is indeed true that he has not travelled very far, but he must not lose hope – his face is still towards me.

Wednesday

The clamour of many different religions confuses humanity. But I have given the wise seeker a start — two sacraments common to all faiths and accessible to every human being without distinction or qualification. They are right at hand, within touching distance. One is the created universe. The other is the saint.

Thursday

Here goes that dear woman again reviling me because she does not know the answers to all the conundrums of life and expects me to tell her. What would she say if I invited her up here where she could see everything? It is strange how everyone wants to be where all is made plain but no one wants to die.

Friday

Another Star Wars film portraying the Devil as the enemy in the universe. But yet again, the author has given him certain admirable qualities. The Devil is always portrayed sympathetically — he is pitiable in his aloneness or tragic in the waste of potentially good qualities or heroic in his last ditch stand against me.

I don't conclude from this that human beings are drawn to the Evil One because they are themselves fundamentally evil. Quite the contrary. They find something sympathetic in the Devil because they are incapable of imagining the wholly evil. It is alien to their basically good natures.

Saturday

Christians do treat their sacred buildings like fortresses. They would rather die than abandon them and join with other Christians just down the road. I do believe if a single Christian were marooned on a desert island he would build *two* chapels, so there was one he didn't want to go to.

·2·

Sunday

These long-winded preachers! They mean well, but I fear their hearers will think I am a very dull deity. What is it about me that evokes such tediousness from some of the righteous?

Monday

I wish insurance companies would stop describing it as an act of God whenever there are floods and natural disasters! That is a very dismal view of my nature. Apparently I only intervene in human affairs when clever people can find no other rational explanation of things that happen to them. They must make up their minds. Either I am in all events or none. If I took special action every time millions of people asked for a favour the world would be in chaos.

The world as a whole depends absolutely on me. But when my children see my hand in some special event, they are saying something very important about themselves rather than me. They are saying that they saw my general will and purpose made plain to them in that event like a glimpse of the sun through a break in the clouds. Or else, like a flash of lightning on a clear day.

Tuesday

Here is a hard customer. He prays, 'O God, if you do not help me, I'll ask my rich uncle in America!' Faced with the threat of the almighty dollar, what can I do?

Wednesday

They have converted a disused church into a bingo hall. The new owners say bingo is a harmless social pleasure. They could not imagine God being unhappy about his now empty house being used to offer company and a little excitement to lonely people. I don't want to be a heavenly wet blanket but I cannot be complacent about the worship of blind chance. That strikes at my very nature. One of my names could almost be anti-chance. I am the essence of what is purposive rather than random in the universe.

Thursday

The church council have dismissed their minister after only six months because of his eccentric habits and his peculiar opinions. Well, he always was a bit of a fool but I've put up with his foolishness for sixty years yet these godly folk couldn't cope with it for six months!

Friday

He engages in anguished inner debate. When ought he to make his peace with me? Well, I can help him there. I don't want to restrict his freedom so let's say he ought to make his peace with me one minute before he dies. Of course, he cannot know when he will die. So he'd better do it now.

Saturday

The philosophers are arguing about my existence again. I have news for them. My bare existence is the least interesting thing about me. Bare existence is boring – ask any cabbage or log of wood. To occupy oneself with arguments about my existence is like sailing the seas to discover an unknown continent, catching sight of it and turning back for home. 'What was it like?' their friends ask. 'No idea,' the explorers reply, 'But it's there all right.'

I have much more interesting things to do than merely exist.

And what can these scholars mean when they talk about my inaccessibility? I am, they claim, elusive. Well, if they can't find me, the reason is simple. They can't find me for the same reason a burglar can't find a policeman.

·3·

Sunday

The faithful few gather in the old church with its peeling paint and rumbling boiler. They try hard to be hopeful as they struggle to keep the doors open and make an impact on their neighbourhood. They should not despair. Those worshippers are dignified beyond their comprehension. They represent the wholeness of my church. If it does not exist in them, it does not exist at all. If the one, universal, holy church is not to be found in that dismal building, it is not to be found anywhere.

Monday

That Yorkshire farmer reminds me of the old Hebrews in his intense sense of place. As he left Matins this morning he bowed his head and said, 'Farewell, Lord, we're emigrating to Australia'.

Tuesday

I can understand the outrage of devout believers at the blasphemies sprinkled throughout modern conversation. But they shouldn't be too upset on my account. Even blasphemy is a back-handed testimony to my existence. I have heard any number of 'God dammits!' and 'Christ almightys!' today but not a single 'Baal dammit!' or 'Woden almighty!' Only a live god gets cursed.

Wednesday

What I choose to give, no one can withhold – so those who rob humanity of my gifts do not long prevail. On the other hand, what I choose to withhold, no one can give – so those who play god are soon revealed as frauds.

Thursday

It is announced in Hollywood that an actor called Mr Charlton Heston is to play me in a new biblical epic. According to the press release, among his qualifications are his craggy good looks, the fact that he has been married to the same wife for many years and that he is President of the Screen Actors' Guild.

I can quite see why they chose him. But some of my best servants wouldn't have such qualifications. Paul was an ugly little man, Abraham was a polygamist and Martin Luther wanted to behead peasants who banded together to form unions. Of course, they were only human whereas I ...

But Hollywood does make it hard for me to live up to their expectations. I recall Mr Cecil B deMille rewriting whole passages of the book of Exodus in order to smooth off some of the rougher corners of my character. I wouldn't wish to upset him, but I did prefer the book to the movie.

Friday

I cannot always give them what they ask for, not because they ask for too much but because they ask for what I do not possess. They cannot have square circles nor wet dryness nor curved straight lines. Nor can they have love without cost, life without pain, truth without effort. I cannot give them what I do not possess.

Saturday

Here's a man who claims he's on this earth by accident and that this accident is just one of an infinite series of accidents going back to the dawn of creation. Just fancy, he's the product of so many accidents! What a terrible insurance risk he must be. I'll bet he didn't get a Christmas card from the Prudential.

• 4 •

Sunday

I'm not too keen on that hymn they're singing – 'Jerusalem, my happy home'. It purports to describe the delights of heaven in such terms as:

> Thy turrets and thy pinnacles
> With precious gems do shine,
> Thy very streets are paved with gold
> Surpassing clear and fine.
>
> Thy gardens and thy gallant walks
> Continually are green
> There grow such sweet and pleasant flowers
> As nowhere else are seen . . .

And so on in the same vein. Christians are such know-alls! I intend heaven to be a lovely surprise for them, but they are already anticipating it as a boring old extension of the Town & Country Planning Act.

Monday

Too many people play games with the Devil, like arm-wrestlers testing their strength. They should leave well alone. It is dangerous, even for playful motives, to contend against one who has nothing to lose.

Tuesday

I rejoice in the creative power of human beings, but it ought to be tinged with modesty. It has its proper limits. They have yet to create a new primary colour or a third sex or another dimension. I permit them to rearrange the basic elements of creation but not to add to them.

16

Wednesday

Some people are fortunate in being naturally good, yet they are still capable of complaining that I show mercy on the wicked. They ought to be grateful the scales of heavenly justice are exquisitely balanced. I have already shown mercy on them in creating them naturally good.

Indeed the good ought never to despise the wicked. Some reprobates please me for reasons the conventionally virtuous could never fathom.

Thursday

Rumour has it that when I banished Lucifer from heaven he was asked what he missed most and he replied, 'The sound of the trumpets in the morning'. It is a fanfare of a different sort that heralds the morning for me.

The nuns troop into chapel for the morning office before it is light. Sister Fortunata shivers in the chill air and she moves very slowly because she is old and cannot see very well. As she lowers herself painfully on to her knees to pray, her arthritic joints crack. That for me is one of the important sounds of the morning – a Te Deum more precious than any words of the liturgy.

Friday

This poor woman is in torment. Again and again she tries to address me and dries up sobbing bitterly because she has lost the power to pray. It matters not. So long as she can weep, I am not much bothered about whether she can pray.

Saturday

A party of American scholars has just returned from Turkey where they claim to have found the remains of Noah's ark on Mount Ararat. According to their measurements, they estimate the ark to have been 173 metres long, 29.7 metres wide and must have weighed over 3 million kilogrammes. I don't understand those measurements. If I had intended the world to go metric would I have chosen twelve apostles?

· 5 ·

Sunday

I do wish that preacher would stop ranting on about history repeating itself. It doesn't. I never do the same thing twice. Every one of my numberless acts of creation is an original, in some way crucially different from all that came before it. So it is fundamentally mistaken thinking on the part of my children when they feel they ought to model themselves on anyone else, however admirable or saintly. I did not create them to be slavish imitations.

So when John Smith stands before me, I won't ask him, 'Why weren't you Moses or Jesus or St Francis of Assisi?' but, 'Why weren't you John Smith?'

Monday

I do understand the problem of unbelievers when, right out of the blue, they receive some blessing that seems utterly miraculous. They remind me of the priest who desecrated the Sabbath by sneaking away to play golf and got a hole in one. He nearly died of frustration because he couldn't tell anyone.

Tuesday

My people are busy in well-doing. They try very hard to keep my commandments and I honour them for their zeal. But the key to any understanding of me does not lie there. The basic commandment is not 'Do this!' or 'Do that!' but 'See!' The essence of religion is not morality but insight. It is not in the disposition to behave correctly but in the capacity to be astonished that our journey together begins.

Wednesday

There really are times when watching the antics of humankind I think I got the order of creation wrong. Perhaps I ought not to have left the creation of men and women to the end of the week when I was tired.

Thursday

More brinkmanship from the great powers. Their plight is now quite novel and utterly pitiable. On the one hand, they face physical annihilation if an enemy uses nuclear weapons against them; on the other, they face moral annihilation if they use nuclear weapons against their enemy.

No nation can now guarantee the safety of its own children: it can only guarantee the safety of its enemy's children and vice versa. Do they have the wisdom to see that?

I wonder . . . do they ever sigh for those far-off days when only I had the power to end the world?

Friday

A scholarly theologian addresses me thus in prayer: 'O thou who art the ground of our being, the paradox of immanent transcendence and transcendent immanence; the Alpha of dynamic inter-personal involvement and the Omega of revelatory historical destiny . . .

Well, I suppose I am. But let's not stand on ceremony. Just use my pet name – Jehovah.

Saturday

What a promising young priest! He is energetic and full of joy. That integrity which is holiness lights up his very face. He is a splendid advertisement for me. But I do wish he would curb his enthusiasm just a wee bit, and when hearing confessions refrain from exclaiming 'Wow!'

·6·

Sunday

Oh dear, we have a pulpit comedian here. So this parson's funny story goes, I am asked by a notorious sinner whether I think he will be able to get his shirt on over his wings when he gets to heaven and I am purported to have replied, 'My friend, where you are going, the question is: will you be able to get your hat on over your horns?' Ha Ha. Pulpit comedians are my pet aversion.

And yet – I do appreciate true wit because it celebrates the unity of creation by joining together things which seem to have no connection. For instance, I permitted myself a smile at Mr Woody Allen's comment, 'Not only is there no God, but it's impossible to find a plumber at the weekend'. Very droll.

Monday

These anxious people ask for a miracle. They do not realize there is nothing to a miracle. If a hundred pious people prayed ceaselessly to a plastic garden gnome, sooner or later, it would be able to perform what they called miracles. Spiritual exhibitionism is the infallible sign of an idol. Subtlety (though I say it myself) is one of the essential qualities of divinity, which is why I planted curiosity in the minds of men and women. They have got to ferret out the truth; it does not hit them over the head through extraordinary happenings.

But I have set myself a problem all the same. One of the greatest needs of my people is to be startled occasionally – they need to echo the first words of the frog in the Garden of Eden – 'Lord, how you made me jump!' But how do I do that and still remain subtle?

Tuesday

Talking of miracles – they call it a miracle if I do what they ask. I call it a miracle if they do what I ask.

Wednesday

It is not humility but the worst arrogance that makes a person think he can sin beyond my power to forgive. He adds one more sin to the rest when he assumes that the magnitude of his sinfulness can exhaust the supply of my mercy. That is a denial of my divinity and therefore it is true atheism.

Thursday

She complains that I seem to be a long way off. So, who has moved?

Friday

Even some of those who believe in me seem to doubt eternity and resign themselves that death is the end. I should have thought their own logic was against them. They could not commune with me now if I did not care for them. They matter to me, and since I am perfect consistency, they cannot cease to matter to me – and therefore they must for eternity.

Or put another way, if I love them at all, I must love them to the end, not their end but my end – hence eternally.

Saturday

A poster in Liverpool reads:

'What will Liverpool do when Christ comes?'

Underneath someone has scrawled:

'Switch Ian Rush to the back four!'

Personally, I'd leave Rush where he is and move Dalgleish. Of course, when Mr Bill Shankly was manager of Liverpool I would not have dared to express an opinion about such matters.

· 7 ·

Sunday

These Christians are so noisy! They pray, preach and sing at me incessantly. Now it is true that in the beginning was the Word – but not words. The universe began not with a big bang but in silence. Everything worthwhile begins in silence.

If we are to be friends, Christians must learn to share the silence of companionship with me before they bombard me with wodges of God-talk. They must know that I am *there* in silent communion before they acknowledge the fact in chatter.

Monday

Often when people pray for miracles they are asking that two and two should not make four. They want me to bend the rules in their case. I wonder ... would they be happy for two and two not to make four when they are travelling at seventy miles an hour on a motorway or flying at 35,000 feet and their lives depend upon mathematical exactitude?

That two and two make four is a sign that the universe is a system and not a chaos. Every time a child counts to ten, he or she salutes the reliability at the heart of things.

Even in the interests of a miracle, do they really want to introduce unpredictability into the centre of their lives?

Tuesday

I long ago made a resolve that humanity was not going to leave the running of the world to me. So, the moment people fold their arms and say 'It's in the hands of God' I just nod off.

Wednesday

What *am* I to do with the Jews? I freely confess they would have had an easier time of it over these past three thousand years if I had not appointed them my chosen people. But they do take advantage! This outraged Jew invokes my aid in cursing his enemy. 'May all your teeth fall out, except one!' he cries. 'Why except one?' asks his enemy, puzzled. 'So you may retain the capacity to suffer toothache' is the lofty reply.

Really! Such impudence is matched only by the Jewish blasphemer who claims he would rather curse me than his enemies because there's only one of me whereas he has many enemies.

I console myself that even Jewish atheists have a sound grasp of theology. They are always monotheists and acknowledge it is indeed *one* God they don't believe in.

Thursday

Humanity is becoming more and more permissive. It is obviously a matter of regret to them that I issued ten commandments rather than ten suggestions.

Friday

A devout, troubled soul is anguished about his sinfulness. I am more worried about the fact he has not taken advantage of the proper human pleasures I have ordained for him. Sins can always be forgiven whereas unlived life is for ever wasted.

Saturday

Sometimes my children are not very wise in the ways of the world. This zealot prays, 'O God, cast down and destroy all the false gods men and women worship in their blindness!' The trouble is – men and women do not only worship useless things like idols of wood and stone but also mighty realities such as the sun and moon and stars. Now, how may I cast down such idols? Am I to destroy part of my own creation because some are deluded enough to worship bits of it?

On the other hand, were I to leave the planets intact but just destroy the idols of wood and stone, the sun, moon and star worshippers would rejoice and cry, 'Verily, ours are true gods because they have not been destroyed!'

· 8 ·

Sunday

What a prodigous pray-er that lay preacher is! His eloquence is breathtaking – the words pour off his tongue in a silver stream; his images are daring and his passion is intense. No wonder the poor man is drenched in sweat by the time he reaches the final 'Amen!'

That must be one of the best prayers ever addressed to a London congregation!

Monday

Not even the redeemed can ever be totally free from sin. Many believers are reduced to despair when having started on the way, confident they have beaten their sins, they stumble and fall. They should take heart – faith in me does not make them unable to sin; it makes them able not to sin.

Tuesday

People make requests of me in prayer as though I had a sort of reserve account of resources, a nest egg under my bed. They do not realize that I have nothing in reserve; I have invested everything I have and am in the universe. Nothing has been held back. It is my pearl of great price on which I have lavished everything.

So, like the poverty-stricken mother of a large family, I can only give more to one of my children by taking something from the others. There are no free lunches in the universe; whatever is taken must be paid for.

Wednesday

O dear! My children are so concerned about matters of rank and status. Here is a group of church dignitaries arguing about who should have precedence in some ecclesiastical ceremony. They ought to remember that in the very first procession – the order of creation – even the lowly flea had precedence over the lot of them.

Thursday

In his anger, he doubts that I am a good God. What other option do I have? The good is defined by what I do.

Friday

A philosopher called Dr Grace Jantzen has written a book called *God's World, God's Body*. It is published by the trinity of Darton, Longman and Todd and has a foreword by the Regius Professor of Divinity at Oxford so it must be taken seriously. Dr Jantzen argues that just as the soul inhabits a body, so I too have a body – which is the physical world.

I confess to some degree of alarm. If the world really is my body then I am in mortal, or rather, immortal danger in the nuclear age since some lunatic might blow it up. Then where should I be?

It is one thing to wipe out humanity – though I'd rather they didn't, given the three billion years of evolutionary pain that has been invested in the most ordinary mortal. As Jesus pointed out, I could at a pinch raise up sons of Abraham from stones (or nuclear dust for that matter). But the very idea of some earthly potentate having the power to obliterate God! These politicians are arrogant enough as it is and need constantly to be reminded that my attributes are not for hire.

Perhaps I should join CND – though I would not wish to embarrass Monsignor Bruce Kent.

Saturday

There is something both sad and funny about human pretensions. Human beings think grand thoughts, nurture huge hopes and long for the unattainable. It is the impress of my image upon them. But so little of it is put into practical effect. People who sigh for immortal life do not know what to do with themselves on a rainy Sunday afternoon. And though they could not create a house fly they invent a new god every week.

·9·

Sunday

I know it is a sign of respect that I am addressed by many believers in sacred languages – languages used for the purposes of worship and no other. It is also claimed that I make my reply by means of 'tongues' – unintelligible noises uttered by believers when they are carried away in spiritual fervour.

But humanity itself is my basic language. Human relationships are the grammar and syntax of my native tongue. There is nothing of overwhelming significance I have communicated to the world in any other way. Or intend to.

Monday

These idol worshippers! I suppose the final proof of my omnipotence is that I don't need to exist in order to save them!

Tuesday

How bitter and angry some theologians get when they quarrel! Their lack of charity towards one another shows they do not understand the first thing about their trade – for love is the abridgement of all theology. All its doctrines, dogmas and propositions tend towards this one, simple end. The theologian who shows no love towards those with whom he is in dispute reveals that he knows absolutely nothing about me, however learned he may be.

Wednesday

In a weak moment I granted that man two wishes – that he would win the football pools and live to be a hundred. Silly of me, I know, but every now and then I have a brainstorm – I'm

27

only superhuman, after all. Well, now he is reviling me for going back on my promises.

He won the pools all right and spent a fair slice of his winnings on a hair transplant, new teeth and cosmetic surgery. Then one day, hurrying out of Harrods, he was knocked down and killed by a taxi. Now he demands to know what happened to the promise that he would live to be a hundred?

To be entirely truthful, he got knocked down because I just didn't recognize him!

Thursday

The impudence of some of my children is beyond belief. This chap prays: 'I know, O Lord, that you will provide, but please advise me who will provide until you do.' He then adds for good measure, 'There are times, Lord, when I think you are more concerned for my salvation than my welfare.'

Friday

A man who failed to catch an aeroplane that subsequently crashed commented, 'Well, as luck would have it, providence was on my side!' I suppose that covers all eventualities.

Saturday

Overheard at a twenty-first birthday party: 'It seems only yesterday that you were a twinkle in your father's eye, lad.' Well, maybe so, but long, long before that the lad was a twinkle in *my* eye.

· 10 ·

Sunday

Believers with a mystical streak use some very daring images
when they are trying to describe me in words. I applaud their
ingenuity, but they do sometimes get carried away. I have just
been described as an inside without an outside and an up
without a down. I ask you!

Within limits I am prepared to be how people perceive me to
be, but even I cannot become that which when put into words
is strictly nonsense. I wish some of the people who write
modern hymns realized this.

Monday

I have no grandchildren.

Tuesday

In that country they amputate a man's hand for theft
and behead a woman caught in adultery. They insist
these punishments are done in my name and they read passages from the holy book whilst the sentences are carried
out.

What strange madness is this! I create human beings whole
for my pleasure and these zealots dismember them to my glory.
They have evolved a new doctrine – salvation by subtraction.
Cut off the hand that steals, pluck out the eyes that lust and
what is left is accounted righteous.

To cut off a man's hand for stealing is as logical as smashing
a musical instrument that plays a false note. If I had wanted to
make it impossible for human beings to sin I would not have
robbed them of their faculties but denied them free will.

Wednesday

I came to the conclusion that I would have to reveal the gospel to men and women because they have neither the time nor the wit to think it up for themselves.

Thursday

She is overwhelmed by her problems and is contemplating suicide. But suicide can only be a temporary solution to her problems. She assumes self-inflicted death is a way *out* of inner pain and does not consider it may be a way *in*.

Apart from anything else, suicide is such a breach of good manners. It is pitching up somewhere, in fact my place, uninvited.

Friday

They enthusiastically acknowledge that my commandments are wise. They all know someone or other to whom they apply.

Saturday

I've been doing the annual accounts. Planet earth is seriously overdrawn. Have her inhabitants looked at the figures lately? Every time a single member is added to the human race earth has to provide an additional fifty-six thousand gallons of milk, nine thousand pounds of wheat and a thousand trees. And the planet must make room for an extra one hundred and fifty thousand pounds of garbage and one hundred and forty thousand pounds of poisonous waste in the atmosphere. And yet they still add millions to their population every day.

The human race is in great danger of accomplishing the most spectacular mass suicide in the history of the universe. They seem incapable of grasping the simple truth that they did not come into the world, they came out of it, and if they do not do what is necessary with the earth, the earth will do what is necessary with them.

At the risk of becoming a heavenly bore, I insist yet again that there are no free lunches in my universe. What human beings take out of the earth they pay for. Or if they don't pay someone else will have to – in this case their children and their children's children.

·11·

Sunday

Remembrance Day. Humanity has this tragic instinct to commit youthanasia every twenty-five years or so. But now in the nuclear age, wars will never again demonstrate who is right (if they ever did); they will only reveal who is left.

It truly astonishes me that souls destined to soar throughout creation without let or hindrance should be put in contention with one another by the accidents of earthly geography. I believe it is called patriotism.

Monday

All the nations seek to recruit me to their cause. They do not seem to realise that not only am I not the enemy of *their* enemies, I am not even the enemy of *my* enemies.

Tuesday

So many of my children are so serious about the problems and challenges of life. Their sense of high purpose is to be applauded; certainly, I can hardly complain about it since I myself gave them dominion over the earth. But as the burdens of achievement lie heavily upon them I do hope they will not forget how to play. For play is a foretaste of the life-style of heaven.

In heaven the question 'What use is it?' has no meaning. It is an earth-bound question. I brought the whole creation into being for my good pleasure, and for no other reason. So play is not just a respite from work but the key to the meaning of the universe.

Heaven is about unhindered laughter, ceaseless joy and liberation from the law of struggle to achieve purpose. In heaven it is always the seventh day of creation when the task of bringing into being gives way to the sheer enjoyment of what is there – a perpetual dancing Sabbath.

In heaven dominion is quite overshadowed by glory.

Wednesday

They ask for guidance but they really seek my corroboration.

Thursday

Good manners decree that one ought not to flaunt one's giving because that robs the gift of grace and the recipient of self-respect.

Even when the price of giving is pain, one ought not to display one's scars. The cost should come home to those for whom the price is paid as though it were their own discovery.

I like to offer a gift in such a way that it seems as though the recipient found it.

Friday

This man rails at me because he claims I have favoured his neighbour who is a believer. He does not realize that I have no power of discrimination in such matters, any more than the sun can withhold its rays from one person and strike the next at will.

If this man has less than his neighbour, it is because he asked for less – not in words but in the disposition of his heart.

Saturday

They are poisoning the atmosphere with exhaust fumes and industrial smoke, polluting the rivers with sewerage and chemicals, tearing down trees in millions and eroding the soil.

It would be bad enough if they owned the earth, but I merely appointed them caretakers. If they go on at this rate, they will become the earth's undertakers.

Sunday

Trinity Sunday today. I derive a certain gentle amusement from observing preachers tie themselves into verbal knots trying to do justice to the complexity of my nature. Of course their troubles start even before they get to the sermon; at the Prayer Book Preface for Trinity Sunday in fact:

> Who art one God, one Lord; not only one Person, but three Persons in one Substance ... without difference or inequality ...

It is a beautifully turned sentence, of course, but I never hear it without wondering – am I really as complicated as all that?

Monday

I do not give my blessing to one person and withhold it from another. All are my beneficiaries. But there is one thing which I cannot confer on any individual, but can only offer to humanity as a whole. It is my Fatherhood. I am only Father to any because I am Father of all. Whoever denies that I am the Father of another human being declares not that other person but himself an orphan.

Tuesday

This scholar claims: 'God will become obsolete in my lifetime.' Well, in *his* lifetime, maybe, but not in *mine*.

Wednesday

The astronauts return to earth after walking on the moon. When they leave the space capsule they must not make direct contact with the earth itself or their fellow human beings until they have been in quarantine. Wearing surgical masks they are whisked off to a totally sterile environment whilst scientists try to discover whether they have brought back any living organism from outer space that might contaminate the earth.

What an incredibly self-centred and negative attitude that is! Anything alien to earth must be presumed to be hostile. Any vestige of foreign life, a wandering microbe or stray enzymic molecule must be destroyed because by definition it must be harmful.

But I created not a single being from the tiniest to the largest whose sole purpose is to cause the death of another creature. Only man invents devices whose sole aim is someone's death.

Thursday

Faith in me ought not to reduce humanity to abject dependence and passivity. For faith is a two-way business. Their faith in me is only one side of the coin; I also repose great faith in them; to this extent – the world belongs to me but it will be what they make it.

Friday

I sympathize with that preacher's attempt to describe my nature and being. Words really will not do. The most one can say, really, is that I am not infinity like an endless mist; I am more a synthesis of infinity and boundary – just as a vast ocean has a near shore. I wonder if that helps?

Saturday

I locate all my mysteries just beyond the range of the human imagination – near enough to tantalize; far enough to extend its range. In a playful mood I tease the human spirit; in a serious mood, I challenge it. Either method makes it grow.

· 13 ·

Sunday

A teenager at youth club prayers addresses me thus:

> God, you have been around a long time
> Even before the hills and trees and stuff like that.
> You've just always been God.
> You make and bust men
> And tell them where to go.
> A thousand years are nothing to you.
> You take care of the bad guys,
> Just like they never was
> Or didn't even last a day.
> We can get hurt if you get mad
> And we just can't hide anything from you.
> We know you check us out real good.
> So God, teach us to wise up
> And get groovy . . .

Thomas Cranmer is appalled but I say: 'Right on, Baby!'

Monday

Their ingenuity in justifying their evil doing is unbelievable. I wonder – when I created humanity did I over-estimate my ability?

Tuesday

In their prayers they ask: 'O Lord, reveal thyself.' They do not know what they ask. The whole purpose of creation is not to reveal me but to hide me; to protect humanity from the impact of a reality too intense to be borne.

So I hide myself from them as an act of mercy, but also as a vote of confidence. If I were to stand over them like an over-bearing guardian they would never grow. I withdraw tactfully so that they have space, room to extend themselves and the freedom to make the inevitable mistakes on the road to maturity.

Were I to paralyse men and women by my presence, they would merge with the lower orders of creation who fulfil themselves through instinctive obedience because they are denied the freedom to do anything else.

Wednesday

Beware of the person who does not fear me. That person is greatly to be feared.

Thursday

I will not do anything for human beings which they are capable of doing for themselves. 'Take it to the Lord in prayer' too quickly becomes a substitute for 'Roll up your sleeves and get on with it!' When a believer is confronted with someone who needs aid, a good rule is for him to act as though I do not exist. He should assume he is the only person in the world who can help.

Friday

Scientists are claiming they are able to manufacture computers that are *almost* human. These machines can already beat the average chess player, compose poetry of a somewhat stilted kind and diagnose diseases. I am most impressed. True, I have not yet heard a computer burst out laughing at the absurdity of human pretensions, but no doubt that will come.

But if these clever chaps ever invent a computer which is as smart as a human being, how will they know? For one sin of the humanly clever is secretiveness; they regard knowledge as power and do not wish to share it. So that as-good-as-human computer would never let on to its inventors that it was their equal.

And in their urge to duplicate my feat in creating people,

these wily scientists have missed the point. I did not just create a person, I created all humanity – all three billion of them. Now, suppose the scientists were able to construct a computer that could do everything a human being is capable of, I imagine it would have to be the size of the British Isles. Then they would have to go on and link it to three billion more of equal size to duplicate what humanity as a whole accomplishes. I doubt they have the time, the space or the money.

The key to my creation is not to be found in the accomplishments of a single human being but in the limitless potential of all humankind acting together – working, loving, forgiving, sacrificing. That is the dream.

The individual is an unfinished work. It is the person-in-community who is the essential genius of my creation. Now, to create one of those artificially is beyond the cleverest of computer scientists – it is a task of (how may I put it delicately?) God-like proportions.

Saturday

The heresy-hunters are in full cry again! It always struck me as rating one's guesses about me very high to burn someone at the stake for not sharing them. And human ideas about me can only be speculation for what I am is humanly unknowable. Of course, what I am *not* any fool can know.

·14·

Sunday

Some of the theologians make very heavy weather of this matter of belief with their dark talk of mortification and self-denial. It really is very simple at the beginning though it gets more challenging as the pilgrimage wears on. To believe in me is to desire greatly that I should exist and live as though I do.

Monday

A mother teaches a child to talk. Now, though that child will have to learn *a* language, she has been born with the capacity to recognize the structure of language. Just as nest-building marks out birds and hive-making is the specific activity of bees, so the power to identify patterns in strings of words is the unique endowment of the human being.

I have made language the key biological endowment of human beings so that solitariness and isolation should be foreign to their nature. Their instinctive feeling for words drives them towards social existence, communion, fellowship.

To choose aloneness and reject human encounter is to render void my distinctive gift of language and so frustrate my creation.

Tuesday

I note they still teach the so-called traditional proofs for my existence in theological colleges. Surely these proofs prove nothing other than the persistence of this idea of my existence . . . if you see what I mean?

Wednesday

It is understandable that human beings should fear death, but it is foolish to describe it as an irrevocable loss – as though mind and spirit should be extinguished for ever. Obviously, matter is not lost – flesh and bone and sinew return to the earth or atmosphere to become the raw material of the future. So . . . would I create a universe in which the lowest is conserved and the highest is allowed to vanish? Would I hang on to dust and ashes and let mind and spirit go?

Thursday

Another nuclear device successfully tested. Perhaps people ought to return the atom to me marked 'opened in error'. No, I gave them dominion so they will live or die by the consequences. And I just wait.

Friday

The evolutionists and the creationists are arguing again about the origins of humanity. They miss the point. The notion of Adam, the one from whom the many emerge, is as important as the reality. When the ancients asked why I created Adam first I offered them several reasons which still apply – so humanity could neither boast about its ancestors nor blame its sinfulness on heredity; so that no-one who came after Adam could claim superiority over another human being on the grounds that he had a more splendid forebear; and so that one common ancestor for all humanity would rule out of court all racialism and nationalism.

And not least, so Adam could not blame his bad temper on any mother-in-law.

Saturday

Writing about me seems to be big business at present. I see a book by Gerald Priestland called *The Case Against God* is on the best seller lists. Where will it all end – with Jesus signing copies of the New Testament at Mowbrays?

·15·

Sunday

At a regimental old comrades' reunion they bewail the fact that their numbers get fewer every year as members die. Well now, if there were an old gods' reunion, how many would attend? Where are those great gods of yesterday, feared and worshipped by millions, now just strange names . . .

Jupiter, for instance. Is there a single worshipper in the entire world who now bows the knee to the Father of the Planets? Or whatsisname . . . Huitzilophchtil god of the Mexicans, in whose honour five thousand youths and maidens were sacrificed in a single day? Or his brother Tpzcatilpoca who consumed twenty-five thousand virgins in a single year and whose thirst had to be slaked by ten thousand gallons of human blood? Where are they now?

Does even the tipsiest Celt now invoke the names of those great Irish gods Dis and Tarves the Bull or Mocos the Pig? Where are Sutekh the big god of the Nile valley or Amon Re, Osiris, Dagon and Molech? Who in his dying breath now calls upon the names of Gunfled, Dagda, Govannon or Robigus? Gone . . . all gone.

It can be a lonely eminence, that of Ancient of Days.

Monday

I think it is just as well that I offer even theologians the gift of eternal life. That should give them just enough time to sort out what they believe about me.

Tuesday

Old Fred lived a life of utter and unrelieved mediocrity. He neither said nor did anything of any significance. He seemed just to occupy space; he related to very few people and even then superficially. Both fervent love and passionate hate were beyond him. He was, then was no more. Death merely put a terminus to his unlived life.

People like Fred make eternal life inevitable. He has got to be given an opportunity to say or do something that justifies the billions of years of evolutionary pain which went into his creation – and the deed that made his salvation possible.

Wednesday

He has suffered the worst fate that can befall a priest or minister. What was once his love has become his business.

Thursday

They pray: 'Heal the sick, comfort the bereaved, feed the starving, give peace in Northern Ireland, the Middle East and Afghanistan. Put an end to strife and division; bring justice to the poor, the discriminated against and the homeless . . .'

Why me? I thought I gave them dominion – which means that the world belongs to me but it will be what they make it.

Friday

He wasn't due here for another two months. He must have had a terrible doctor.

Saturday

She proudly claims to be an atheist but confesses she knows nothing of the Bible or any other sacred book. Nor has she gone to the trouble of finding out what worship and prayer are all about. She is not an atheist, she is an ignoramus.

·16·

Sunday

A lay preacher offers public prayer:

'O Lord, thou knowest that we have come here to praise thee. Thou knowest, too, that each of us comes with his own burden of sins and sorrows. Thou knowest what they are because our innermost hearts are open to thy gaze. Thou knowest too the problems we face as a nation – rising unemployment, the miners' strike, the floods on the East coast. And Lord, thou knowest too that we have no right to be here because we have failed thee ... We have refused the means of grace, staying away from public worship, not saying our prayers. Lord, thou knowest ...'

Indeed, I do. Now, either tell me something I don't know or stop wasting my time with gossip.

Monday

I created them in my own image. They have returned the compliment with a vengeance.

Tuesday

John Calvin and his doctrine of the total depravity of man continues to cause much misery. He is a doctor and a saint so his views should not be lightly discounted. Let's settle for a theological compromise and agree that man is vile but people are wonderful.

Wednesday

The philosophers spend too much time wrestling with ultimate issues. Some questions are so big that they are rendered unimportant by their magnitude. It's like arguing about the weight of the Alps to the nearest million tons. It is by their response to simple, practical questions that people live or die.

Thursday

A devout Jew was climbing Mount Carmel. His foot slipped and he hung over a sheer drop by clinging to the branch of an overhanging tree. I responded to his cry for help by asking him whether he trusted me without reservation. He said he did, so I told him to let go of the branch. 'What?' he asked. 'Let go of the branch' I repeated. There was a pause, then he asked, 'Excuse me, but is there anyone else up there?'

Friday

My judgment of people is bound to differ from that of my children. They see only what other people do. I see why.

Saturday

I know I created everything good but I could swear I detect a crack in the universe – caused, no doubt, by expansion due to the volume of hot air rising from all those pulpits.

·17·

Sunday

I still reflect ruefully upon Adam's fall from grace. He had an unrepeatable destiny. No-one had ever thought his thoughts before him, so he was a true genius. None of his actions was a slavish imitation of the behaviour of others. Nowhere in his character was there the taint of hereditary weakness. In a unique way he was his own man. Yet he threw it all away to share the imperfect knowledge of general humankind. That was his tragedy and his glory.

Monday

He stands alone against the crowd, a solitary voice crying the truth in the teeth of a howling gale of lies and calumny. He should not despair. It is true that alone he is in a minority of one. But together, he and I constitute a majority.

Tuesday

I accept the atheist's compliment, though I know he does not intend it. What he is saying is that my creation is so perfect that he can dispense with the Creator.

Wednesday

Indeed, the theologians do have a problem. According to any human system of logic I can be either all powerful or perfect, but not both. As all powerful I would be irresistible; as perfect, the merest child could resist me because I could not coerce her.

Thursday

There is a curious notion on earth that I treat the good and the wicked differently when they finally stand in my immediate presence. How could I? I have and am only love. What is called my judgment is not some exercise in supernatural accountancy but exposure to my love. So the good may discover how partial and egotistical their own love is and feel penitence and gratitude. The wicked, because they cannot be at peace with my love, find themselves in a state not of utter torment but complete incomprehension, faced with a love they can neither evade nor live with.

That state is called hell because for the wicked stuck in an environment irradiated by love is like being a fish that cannot stand water.

Friday

Though human beings could be described as my creatures, they have one absolute power which I cannot overcome. Though I created them without their consent I cannot redeem them without it.

Saturday

People truly have a distorted sense of economy. They could get to heaven with half the effort they invest in going to hell.

·18·

Sunday

You could say I created the universe as an act of mercy. It is as though all the possibilities of creation burned with desire to come into existence and I gave them release.

Monday

Of course I could yield to their entreaties and reveal to them all the mysteries of nature and of humankind. But then they would wither and die of boredom.

Tuesday

It is by the names I am called that needs of my people are known and their religious history is revealed. My Muslim children have ninety-nine such names; they tell them daily on their rosary beads.

Benefactor	He who opens
King	He who shuts
Prophet	He who sees
Judge	He who answers
Healer	He who raises
Conqueror	He who lowers
Defender	He who gives dignity
Prince	He who holds good
Lord of Majesty	He who divides them
Lord of Generosity	He who distributes them
Master of Death	He who takes it away
Creator	He who produces
Protector	He who unites
Guardian	He who anticipates
Merciful	Beauty

Attentive

Faithful

Subtle

Observer

Great

Fruitful

Glorified

Magnificent

Master

Giver

Dispenser

Generous

Sentinel

Splendid

Invincible

Praiseworthy

Resurrection

Abundant

Immutable

Eternal

Charity

First

Revealed

Most Excellent

Witness

Strong

Forgiveness

Good

Kingdom

Sufficient

Light

Glorious

Guide

Sublime

Sweetness

Peace

Just

Mighty

Clement

Magnanimous

Pleasing

Vigilant

Indulgent

Bestower

Providence

Majestic

Knowledge

Wise

Most loving

Holy

Omniscient

Living

New

Unique

Goodness

Prudent

Last

Hidden

Omnipotent

Truth

Righteous

Justice

Lovable

Equitable

Rich

Compassionate

Universal

Perfect

Patient

Wednesday

And there is a hundreth name. Whoever cries out to me in extremity I will answer whatever name he calls me.

Thursday

I have concluded that the reason theologians are prone to the fault of self-importance is that they tend to confuse my truth with their formulations of it. It is one of the characteristics of my truth that its existence does not depend upon *anyone* believing it.

Friday

Because the Devil was originally one of my creatures I have many advantages over him. One is this – I can imagine what it is like to be the Devil; he cannot imagine what it is like to be God.

Saturday

It is understandable that my servants should wish to live at peace with all people and to avoid unseemly behaviour and loud controversies. Indeed, much of the business of the Kingdom is transacted in secret. Nevertheless, they must nerve themselves to realize that there are times when a great work for me will have the earth in uproar and the legions of hell baying for their prey.

·19·

Sunday

Of course, I appreciate proper humility in my children but there are times when they overdo it. Their prayers of confession so easily become exercises in self-indulgence. If they are not investing their rebelliousness with a tragic grandeur more suited to fallen angels than ordinary human beings, they are belittling themselves in ways that, by implication, belittle me – as though I were capable of creating rubbish.

Monday

A ringing testimonial from an awesome source. According to a recent biography, Field Marshal Viscount Montgomery, the British Second World War leader, once began a speech, 'As God has said, and I think, rightly . . .'

Tuesday

My children do find it hard to keep some sense of proportion about the created order. They are either carried away by its splendours into some kind of nature worship or else recoil from its cruelties and turmoil into a world-denying spiritism. Nature is only a first sketch of that glory of the new creation which will be revealed when earth and suns and stars have passed away. Therefore it should be respected but not idolized. It has some perfections because it is *my* image; but it also has imperfections because it is only my *image*.

Wednesday

I am being lobbied frantically on all sides on the issue of whether the Church of England should ordain women as priests. The nub of the argument seems to be that since Jesus was a man, only men can be priests. Of course, Jesus was a man but he wasn't a priest; he was also Jewish, bearded and wrote in the dust with his left hand (a fact never before revealed). I confess that what the theologians call his incarnation was not intended to encourage slavish imitation of the detail of his becoming man but the free and creative association of one spirit with another.

When priests stand before the altar, the matters which concern me are these: are we at peace, so that there is nothing between us, no shadow upon our relationship? Do they know their sins to be finally and fully forgiven?

Are they content to be servants and ready for sacrifice of spirit as well as life? In a word, are they new creatures in Christ? If so, their original gender is of no more account than the vestments they put on and take off.

I fear this will sadden the heart of my loyal servant, the Bishop of London, but I trust he will take his disappointment like a . . . well, like a man.

Thursday

A television discussion about whether it is possible for people to be happy without me. Of course they can. They can be happy without me, but since they cannot *be* without me, such happiness is based on illusion.

Friday

An example of justification by faith that would delight my servant Martin Luther. One finds theologians in the strangest places! An old reprobate rises to his feet in a Methodist class meeting and confesses, 'You all know me. I'm a drunk and a wife-beater. I neglect my children, steal from my friends and gamble away my dole money. But thank God I ain't never lost my religion!'

Saturday

My mercy rests in this fact. I know men and women better than they know themselves and never inflict upon them all I know they are capable of enduring.

· 20 ·

Sunday

Philosophers are a hardy band. I admire both their ingenuity and their scepticism. They keep at this matter of my existence; generation after generation, they doggedly address the problem. They are doomed to frustration. No rational explanation can be given for my nature because my nature is the ground of rationality.

Monday

The theological gossip columnists have been writing about me again. Thus, Dr Thomas Altizer in *The Gospel of Christian Atheism*: 'The death of God is a final and irrevocable event, and God's death has actualized in history a new and liberated humanity.'

Me, dead? I don't even feel ill.

Tuesday

Human beings must be known to be loved. I must be loved to be known.

Wednesday

I must confess that after the creation of the universe I felt *anything* else that happened must be an anti-climax. Then came Calvary – which truly shook the foundation of things. There remains the end, the consummation. The heavenly life is one of eternal placidity punctuated by the reverberations of world-shattering historical events.

Thursday

Talking of the consummation ... I do wish people would stop trying to predict when it will happen. They've been trying to second-guess me ever since Paul had to put the Thessalonians right about it. Believers at least should realise that its utter unpredictability is central to the significance of the event. If, for argument's sake, Pastor O'Reilly were to tell his congregation that having studied the Book of Revelation he was in a position to announce that end of the world would take place the following Thursday at four o'clock in the afternoon, and if he happened to hit on the correct date and time, I should be involved in some very inconvenient reorganization.

The moment at which the heavens roll up like a scroll must remain totally unguessable, so that believers will always take into account its possibility and 'sit loose' to their lives as precarious and provisional. They should not give their whole heart to anything which will end when life or even history does.

Friday

A couple at odds who cannot possibly achieve reconciliation because though both have come to the meeting prepared to forgive, neither is prepared to be forgiven.

Saturday

What clever beings humans are! They have mastered the winds, waves, the tides, gravity. When they succeed in harnessing the power of my love, for the second time in history they will have discovered fire.

·21·

Sunday

All intelligent minds love puzzles. I am no exception. I know that if I exert myself and ransack my memory I can recall *anything*, but I prefer to toy with some apparent mysteries mostly to do with my past decisions and actions. For instance, why did I find Abel's worship more acceptable than that of Cain? Why, though the Bible is my Word, is there not a single mention of me in the Book of Esther? Why did I settle on boils and not some more heroic affliction to torment Job? Why do tomb-stone inscriptions combine the most indubitable truths with the worst possible taste? How did I know when I endowed the human species with ears that a billion years later bishops would need them to keep their mitres from tilting over their eyes? Why do I go on claiming responsibility for such an absurd world?

Monday

The heresy hunters are at work again on my behalf, so they claim. Leaving aside the fact that all great truths begin as heresies, a heresy is a sudden explosion of faith whose energies have not yet been subdued into the smooth, well-worn conduits of official doctrine. It is, therefore, not always to be deplored.

Tuesday

Of course, there are heresies and heresies ... Astrology must be at least three thousand years old and it still retains its hold on the popular imagination through newspaper star columns and television gurus. Human beings ought to be profoundly grateful they are not at the mercy of a fate determined by the mechanical movements of matter which is of a lower order of creation than they are. Can they imagine what life would really be like if their futures were fated? If they were fated to drown, even a glass of water would be full of menace; if they were fated to suffocate, they could choke on a crumb of bread, and if fate decreed that they would perish in the claws and teeth of wild beasts, they could be savaged to death by a flea.

Wednesday

Someone who is truly penitent has little to say for himself. He usually stands before me in silence. Which is well, because it has been my experience that penitents prepared to recall in detail their past sins are capable of repeating them.

Thursday

He says he believes in nothing. How lucky he is that at least two people believe in him – his wife and myself.

Friday

Heated argument on television about whether it is necessary to go to church in order to worship me. One well-tanned hedonist insists that he can worship me just as easily on the golf course. And so he can, if he imagines that I am pleased by prayers whose spiritual and intellectual content is of the order, 'O God, don't let me miss this putt!'

Saturday

This whole line about humanity being a speck of dust in the vastness of the cosmos, totally insignificant and powerless wearies me. Human beings have an ultimate form of power. I predestined them to salvation, the Devil would like to pre-destine them to damnation – and they have the casting vote.

·22·

Sunday

As the author of the Book of Genesis so truly pointed out, in the beginning was a void. I created the whole universe out of nothing. And when I eavesdrop on some sermons, I fear the nothingness shows through.

Monday

The sceptics complain that the world is getting worse; that history is a downward spiral into ever-greater disaster and evil. Many older Christians seem to think the same. Things are not as they used to be, they moan. They certainly aren't. They should have my memory! Things getting progressively worse? Why, when Adam had the whole world to himself and only one commandment to keep, he still broke it. Then there were Cain and Abel . . . You would imagine that the earth was big enough for two people to be able to live in peace – but one ends up murdering the other. So, given, (what?) three thousand million inhabitants of the present-day world, I wouldn't say the sinfulness is proportionately greater.

Tuesday

Humans generally seem to think I'm pretty hard on them. Believe me, there are some people I'm flattering just by enduring them at all.

Wednesday

Another awful earthquake. It's amazing how I always get dragged into discussion about natural calamities even by people who wouldn't give me a thought at any other time. Why do I allow it to happen, they demand? It's a one-sided question. If I were to interfere when things are going well for people, and limit their freedom in any way, they would scream that I was treating them as less than fully responsible human beings. Those aren't the rules you laid down, they'd protest. So true. I created human beings not as puppets on a string but as free spirits, with no divine interference where either the kicks or the ha'pennies of life are concerned. So ... because the world isn't a piece of clockwork where cause and effect are precisely related, humanity is bound to get benefits it hasn't earned and suffering it hasn't deserved. Aggrieved moralists should console themselves with the knowledge that if their virtues sometimes go unrewarded, so too their vices often escape punishment. At least, in history.

Thursday

Even in this sceptical age, if a believer talks to me it is called prayer; if he claims he heard me speaking to him in return, they call it schizophrenia and haul him off for treatment.

Friday

A hard God, me? I am returning good for evil all the time. And in the most obvious ways. When my children harbour thoughts about me which are not worthy of them, I return the compliment by putting into their heads thoughts of which they are not worthy.

Saturday

A ringing declaration at a church assembly by a bishop who seems overtly dogmatic about his faith. He is really talking about his belief rather than his faith. It's belief and not faith when someone else has done the thinking.

· 23 ·

Sunday

They pray to me for the peace of the world *and* spend much of their substance on sophisticated weapons of war. If they are not mocking me by such prayers, what precisely are they asking me to do? They may trust in the Bomb, that is prudent; they may trust in me, that is risky but a genuine option. But to distribute trust judiciously between myself and the Bomb is to place me in alliance with what even they acknowledge is evil. That is a particularly deadly form of blasphemy.

Monday

When human beings contend with one another, man to man, in sport or war, it does not matter which of them wins, I always suffer, for whoever loses always curses me.

Tuesday

Believers have a special contempt for hypocrites. Well, one cannot help having a wee bit of admiration for thorough-going hypocrites; it's such a demanding job, requiring constant vigilance. You can be a murderer or adulterer in your spare time, but it's a full-time occupation being a true hypocrite. Even then I think a hypocrite is to be preferred to a certain kind of person who prides himself on his frankness and plain speaking. He claims to be totally candid, but he isn't really because he is hiding his secret pleasure in speaking truths that are unpleasant.

Wednesday

If the wicked ever got together and acted in concert they could overwhelm my world. Luckily, the same instincts that set them at odds with the rest of humanity also drive them into competition with each other.

Thursday

A group of rather crabbed elders opine that it is the Devil who tempts the young to enjoy themselves.

I suppose that must be the same Devil who tempts the old to condemn the young for their enjoyment. The Devil seems to keep everyone happy – the young get enjoyment from their pursuits and the old from condemning them.

Friday

As I've explained before – nothing and nobody can be totally evil, evil through and through. In this sense, good and evil are not equal qualities. You can have the wholly good but not the wholly evil, for even that which is regarded as evil through and through can only be wholly evil in its *attributes*; it's nature must be good because I created it.

Saturday

As the Sabbath starts, a poor Jew finds himself in the woods without his prayer book. He addresses me as follows: 'Dear God, I have done a stupid thing: I do not have my prayer book with me, and being an uneducated man with a poor memory, I cannot recite the prayers by heart. But you know all the prayers, Lord ... so I'll recite the letters of the alphabet and you put them together in the way you think best.' And this he proceeds to do. And it is, from him, a very acceptable prayer.

Sunday

There is a prudent element in all religion. Deep beneath all the rituals, liturgy and fine sentiments there lurks a desire to domesticate me, to turn away in advance my wrath. It is the tragic illusion of the earnestly religious that they not only think this possible but also that they have accomplished it. They begin to treat me as though I were a great cuddly moth-eaten lion without teeth. I can tell when they lose their respect and begin to presume – their imagery gets less primitive and their language more philosophical; fear gives way to urbanity. I cease to be the hissing serpent or ravening wolf or swooping eagle and become the ground of being or the unmoved mover or the great first cause – titles to be argued about rather than to instil awe.

Let my children beware when they begin to treat me like their old pal upstairs. It's not much fun being turned into a pillar of salt.

Monday

I can't be getting older, that is not possible, but I seem to spend longer and longer listening to people who haven't got anything to say.

Tuesday

Humanity's understanding of me was transformed when it was realised that to reconcile my power and my love is not a philosophical conundrum – the only power I possess is that of my love. Of course, it took Calvary to make the point indisputably.

Wednesday

The desires of my children do not necessarily become respectable because they offer them to me in prayer. Prayer is the purification of desire. It is not only pointless but unintelligent to entertain a thousand desires when there is only a handful of choices.

Thursday

Whoever takes one step towards me, I will take ten steps towards him.

Friday

A great university has just awarded a distinguished cleric the degree of Doctor of Divinity. What a curious title; shall we soon see the appointment of Professors of Humility and Senior Lecturers in Repentance? I confess I have considerable problems in knowing how to respond to these ecclesiastical titles. How much reverence makes the difference between the Right Reverend, the Most Reverend and the Very Reverend? They're all miserable sinners and precious children to me. I know of no way of measuring degrees of reverence. Still, I suppose these little courtesies are some compensation for low pay.

Saturday

To the Christian, the Jew seems to be the blindly stubborn believer who cannot see the change that has come over the world through Jesus; to the Jew, the Christian is the bafflingly daring believer who insists in an unredeemed world that its redemption has been accomplished. They are two zones of faith with a common centre – me, and the outward ripples of their influence mingle and unite and augment one another.

· 25 ·

Sunday

This preacher speaks, a little proudly, I suspect, of his love of 'wrestling' with me in prayer. What can that mean – that I am reluctant to act in certain ways and need to be persuaded to change my mind; that the fate of some person or issue depends on the eloquence and forensic skill of whoever is praying; or that prayer-wrestling is a divine hobby I share with believers, a little like golf? There is no question of my changing my mind. The change occurs in the minds of the believers who are praying. As they are bound to me in concern for the person for whom they are praying so the work of love is done. So it is not so much expostulation or agonized supplication as calm contemplation that is the healthiest attitude for prayer – they should imaginatively reflect on my relationship to those for whom they are praying.

Monday

Why don't I compel the godless to believe, cries one frustrated Christian? Quite simply because compulsion produces hypocrites not disciples.

Tuesday

The inadequacies of human language cause all manner of theological problems. For instance, the sincere desire to possess me is not like the desire to possess material goods or even another person. To desire gold and actually to have it are two very different things. But to desire me earnestly *is* to possess me.

Wednesday

The problem with a certain scientific temper of mind is that the one who possesses it understands less than he knows. The truly religious mind understands more than it knows. It therefore has room for mystery.

Thursday

I heard an Irish toast the other day that expresses a certain profound if picturesque truth: May you get to heaven half an hour before the Devil knows you're dead.

Friday

There is no point in human beings who bewail natural calamities looking around for divine scapegoats. For them to have dominion, as I have often said, means that the world belongs to me but it will be what he or she makes of it. It may be a hard truth, but what human beings don't do through their own dedicated efforts and combined talents to stave off natural calamities or ameliorate their worst consequences, won't get done at all. Then, why pray to me about such things? – in order that I may share their anguish and channel my love through them. For what other agency do I possess to influence the life of the world? I have foresworn lightning and thunderbolts and withdrawn angels since Pentecost.

Saturday

They pray for the welfare of countries they cannot even find on the map – so little are they prepared for the intellectual cost of intercession. A catalogue of the world's trouble spots may be an expression of vacuous good but it is not true prayer.

Sunday

This believer prays that the people of a particularly remote and dangerous part of the world might hear the good news of the gospel. Is he prepared to be the answer to his own prayer? It is always dangerous to make such requests because it is my rule, other things being equal, that those who pray for difficult and costly things should be the agency by which their prayers are accomplished. Apart from anything else, it is so much more economical to use one who is already siezed of the challenge than to start from scratch stirring up someone else.

Monday

Observing the behaviour of some of my children towards one another, I have reached the sad conclusion that the Devil must be the supreme optimist if he thinks he can tempt human beings into even greater meanness than they are capable of showing at present.

Tuesday

'He was content to be a humble believer and a sound if not original theologian' – extract from an obituary. There is a contradiction in terms there. The essence of originality is not novelty but sincerity. A theologian or anyone else is original not because he has remarkable thoughts or particularly profound beliefs but because such beliefs as he has are his own – he believes for himself and for no one else.

Wednesday

It is not particularly flattering to be told that I am the product of human ingenuity, a creation of the inspired or diseased human mind. Really, the logic of it! To claim that without human beings I would not exist is like saying that without maggots there would be no meat.

Thursday

I have no wish to denigrate the courage and loving spirit of the true humanist. But it seems to me that for the humanist to propose blueprints for ameliorating the human condition is like the patient writing his own prescription.

Friday

If a believer is called away from an act of worship in order to help some fellow human being in need, he must go immediately and without any sense of impiety. I can always get angels to chant my praises but only my children can do acts of charity.

Saturday

Another devotee of the blank cheque school of prayer. She prays 'Thou knowest best what is for the good of the world and of your children, so we pray simply thy will be done . . .' This is not spiritual acceptance but secular irresponsibility. If I had intended the whole creation to be by definition incapable of resisting my will, I would not have made beings able to be disobedient in the first place. I wish my will to be done through them and in specific ways. That is the point. In a fallen world, some things are possible and others are not. And it is for those who pray to discover the difference. The rhythm of prayer is like the rhythm of discipleship – action and contemplation, militancy and acceptance, courage and serenity. The truly mature disciple knows where the one merges into the other. And prayer helps to clarify the matter.

· 27 ·

Sunday

I get no particular pleasure from observing one part of my creation do with difficulty what another part can do with ease. Hence, I derive as much satisfaction from the bird that flies effortlessly as from the man who manages to get into the air with much difficulty and ingenuity. The point is that the bird in flying is fulfilling the law of its being, whereas it is not the law of man's being to fly. He must show forth my glory by living like a man and not a bird.

Monday

I can tell by the very way he handles the Bible that he is not searching for enlightenment but looking for loopholes.

Tuesday

My relationship to my children is inevitably full of paradox; in the game of life I am not the solution but the riddle. Men and women can neither fully know me nor ever escape me. I can neither be found nor evaded. They seek me vainly, but I find them: when they try to evade me I haunt them. The theologians who can always find a word for most things call me 'ineluctable'. It is a quality that adds tang to my dealings with my children. If I were completely undiscoverable they would lose interest and abandon the search; if I were simply inescapable, they would eventually through familiarity begin to ignore me. As it is, there is no certainty in the relationship, no possession beyond any shadow of doubt – otherwise faith would be an irrelevance and unbelief sheer madness.

Wednesday

This prince of the church is a good man and a faithful servant. He has however a touch of vanity and should beware lest he loses through pride what he has gained by grace.

Thursday

They never learn the chief lesson of war; again and again, they fall into the old trap – they start wars in the hope that their nation will be better off; when that becomes questionable they fight on in the hope that their enemy will end up worse off; then have to settle for the satisfaction that he isn't any better off than they are. Finally, the post-mortem reveals infallibly that everyone is worse off.

Friday

There is a sense in which it is worse for a human being to sin against a fellow human being than against me. For the one harmed may, in the flux of life, move off to an unknown place, where it is impossible to beg his forgiveness. I, however, am everywhere and so can always be found when one of my children wishes to speak to me words of contrition.

Saturday

I created the universe not in order to acquire something but in order to give it away. Hence, I do not like that phrase in the Burial Service 'The Lord gave, the Lord taketh away ...' What I give, I never take back. Nor do I need to take back one of my children who has died. He never left me.

· 28 ·

Sunday

I've had an end of term report in an anthology of the things scholars have been writing about me lately. Alas, I'm revealed as a below-average deity. Jean Paul Sartre speaks of my 'silence', Heidegger, of my 'absence', Jaspers, of my 'concealment', Martin Buber, of my 'eclipse', W.H. Auden, of my 'distance', Paul van Buren, of my 'meaninglessness', Tillich, of my 'non-being', Nietzsche, of my 'death'.

Still, I know a greengrocer who speaks eloquently of my love.

Monday

Not even I can rewrite the past, yet the historians are doing it all the time.

Tuesday

Too many believers gossip about me and call it prayer or preaching. They confuse loquacity with communication. In the beginning I uttered only one Word – Jesus – in the silence before creation. Any noble design, beautiful work or great endeavour matures in patient silence before it speaks out in its accomplishment. All the high points of my communication with my creation have been acts of silence. So communication becomes communion; the gap between speakers and listeners is not just bridged but transcended.

Wednesday

What my children call miracles are not breaches of the rules; they do not violate natural law. A miracle *is* the natural law of a unique event.

Thursday

The greatest spiritual danger of the present time is the condition described by Jesus as blasphemy against the Holy Spirit. He warned men and women on my behalf that this was the sin that was unforgiveable even though those who sinned against the Son of Man might be forgiven. What he meant of course is that someone might be forgiven for not being able to believe in every dot and comma of Christian theology or even for not being recognizably Christian. But there is no hope for anyone who makes light of that spirit which the common conscience of humanity, whatever its creed, recognizes as divine. This is not godlessness but something much more dreadful, the constitutional inability to be religious at all. To use the language of the biologist, I fear a society is being created which the God-gene has been bred out of.

Friday

They must learn to wait. This is what fervent believers find it hardest to do. It is easier for them to engage in strenuous effort or costly sacrifice or heroic discipleship for my sake than it is for them to wait. Their inability to wait is not just human impatience, it is also a false perception. They feel no need to wait for me because they imagine they already have me imprisoned within a doctrine or pressed between the leaves of a holy book or enclosed within an ecclesiastical structure. They must learn to wait.

Saturday

This politician has sub-titled his autobiography, 'The Memoirs of a Self-Made Man'. At least, that relieves me of an onerous responsibility.

· 29 ·

Sunday

I see the crux of their problem. They are trying to work upwards from their experience to me ... from nature to my glory; from human love to divine tenderness; from their personal history to my actions. They must learn to work downwards. They must not try to deduce from life what I am like but learn from me what life is intended to be. They must not try to think human thoughts divinely but divine thoughts humanly. Of course, the truth will be realized by experience but it does not proceed from experience. Faith must be their relationship to what possesses them and not to what they possess.

Monday

Adam was the only man who never suffered from that most baffling of human afflictions, fluff in the navel. But that was a small consolation for bringing about the fall of man.

Tuesday

This refreshingly modest woman doubts that she would ever have the courage to be my servant – she fears doubt, indifference, difficulty and even martyrdom. There is only one form of courage needed to be a believer; that is the courage to live by grace.

Wednesday

Why will some of my followers get themselves into such a state about the date of the end of the world? Here is a silly preacher who claims to have fathomed it out using diagrams constructed from playing about with chapters of the Book of Revelation.

An attempt to prove the unknowable by means of the unintelligible – the disease of the biblical literalist and vendor of holy relics alike.

Thursday

An American university has just published a fifty-volume history of the human race. I can save busy people a lot of time by providing them with a three-sentence summary of the lessons to be learned from human history. I made human beings mortal; that is their fate. They refuse to accept this mortality; that is their sin. They are brought low; that is their punishment. All the rest is padding.

Friday

Why did I make love of the brethren the test of love for me? Simple. Whilst someone might be genuinely unsure about his love for me, he *knows* beyond a shadow of a doubt whether he loves his neighbour or not.

Saturday

The belief in immortality does not rest in philosophy; it is not to be located in any organism, physical or psychic, but in a relationship with me. What human beings call immortality, life beyond death, is a gift; it is due to my incessant gift and creation. I do not offer anyone an indefinite lease of life at the beginning as a right. They go on solely because they are in communion with me. You might say that someone is immortal because I have need of him or her – and my needs, like my attributes, are everlasting. Immortality is not a riddle; it is a destiny.

· 30 ·

Sunday

The only form of omniscience that is possible within history is self-sacrifice. It is an ultimate form of power because it depends upon no one else's favour, help or agency. In this one thing it is possible to have absolute authority; it is an utterly sovereign act. One may not be able to choose the place or the time or the means but one can choose the end. The greatness of an act is measured by the degree of self-surrender involved. That is why Calvary is the point in history at which my omniscience was decisively demonstrated.

Monday

Here is a congregation in a great state over their minister whom they have discovered in some minor but faintly scandalous fault. The problem with some lay folk is that they think they pay a minister to be good on their behalf. They expect him or her to be a walking Sunday.

Tuesday

My servant Pascal said that I am not the God of the philosophers. Well, I am to this extent. Philosophy can define the limits of the knowable; the true philosopher knows what he cannot know. Once he has reached the limits of rational knowledge, the nonsense can be left behind and the great adventure begin. So the philosopher is a trail-blazer, and provided he seeks the truth and serves the good he will realise his honourable vocation.

Wednesday

They need fear only one thing – the loss of my friendship.

Thursday

These scientists have lost the poetic spirit which alone can illuminate the mystery underlying all things. They say, for example, that the sun rises because of the rotation of the earth. Nonsense! The sun rises because I say to it, 'Come on then, get up!' The fact the stars twinkle has nothing to do with their gaseous nature. The stars twinkle because I urge them, 'For my sake, smile!'

Friday

It is a great tragedy for anyone to go into eternity with possibilities which that person has prevented from becoming actualities. For a possibility is a hint from me.

Saturday

I deny no man peace except to give him glory.